H. Richard Steinhoff

Real Estate Investing 101

Best New Foreclosure Solutions, Top 10 Tips

REAL ESTATE INVESTING 101

Best New Foreclosure Solutions, Top 10 Tips

By H. Richard Steinhoff

© 2015 H. Richard Steinhoff. All rights reserved.

No part of this material may be used, reproduced, distributed or transmitted in any form and by any means whatsoever, including without limitation photocopying, recording or other electronic or mechanical methods or by any information storage and retrieval system, without the prior written permission from the author, except for brief excerpts in a review.

This book is intended to provide general information on real estate only. Neither the author nor publisher provides any legal or other professional advice. If you need professional advice, you should seek advice from the appropriate licensed professional. This book does not provide complete information on the subject matter covered. This book is not intended to address specific requirements, either for an individual or an organization. This book is intended to be used only as a general guide, and not as a sole source of information on the subject matter. While the author has undertaken diligent efforts to ensure accuracy, there is no guarantee of accuracy or of no errors, omissions or typographical errors. Any slights of people or organizations are unintentional. Any reference to any person or organization whether living or dead is purely coincidental. The author and publisher shall have no liability or responsibility to any person or entity and hereby disclaim all liability, including without limitation, liability for consequential damages regarding any claim, loss or damage that may be incurred, or alleged to have been incurred, directly or indirectly, arising out of the information provided in this book. Names and identifying details have been changed, and some of the stories have been recreated.

About the Author

During his 30 years as a real estate broker, H. Richard Steinhoff has been involved in thousands of transactions with buyers, sellers, and investors. This gives him a unique perspective, because he can speak from experience "in the trenches." He is also author of the best-selling book, **"Turning Myths Into Money: An Insider's Guide to Winning the Real Estate Game."**

Richard's education includes a Bachelor of Science degree in Business Administration from California State University, and a Certificate in Business from UCLA Graduate School of Business.

His real estate background includes serving as president of the ERA Broker Council, president of the Broker Council of Southern California, vice-president and director of the Board of Realtors, director of the California Association of Realtors, as well as membership in the National Association of Realtors.

Richard has appeared on numerous talk radio shows from coast-to-coast, as well as television news programs, including Fox News in Los Angeles.

He has received the "Man of the Year" Award from the Chamber of Commerce, the President's Award from the Muscular Dystrophy Association, and has been listed in *"Who's Who in California"* as well as *"Who's Who in the*

West." He was recently designated "Honorary Member for Life" by the California Association of Realtors for distinguished service. He has also received a "Certificate of Recognition" from the California State Legislature. Richard holds a CIBN and CSS designations and is a member of the American Mensa Society.

He is an avid golfer, amateur magician, and a veteran of the U.S. Marine Corps.

TABLE OF CONTENTS

Real Estate Investing 101 --- 2

About the Author --- 4

Introduction -- 7

Tip # 1: Can You Make Money by Buying Bank Repossession (REO)? -- 8

Tip # 2: Are Foreclosed Homes Found Only in Bad Neighborhoods? -- 13

Tip # 3: When Buying a House during the Foreclosure Process, is It Best to Buy in the Pre-Foreclosure Position? - 14

Tip # 4: Will a Foreclosure Adversely Affect Your Credit? --- 16

Tip # 5: Do Foreclosed Homes Always Need a Lot of Work? 18

Tip # 6: Do Foreclosures Affect your Ability to Buy Another House? -- 20

Tip # 7: Does a Homeowner Has a Redemption Period after a Foreclosure Sale Where He Can Regain Title to His Home? 21

Tip # 8: Can I Stay in My House for 30 Days after the Bank Has Repossessed It? -- 22

Tip # 9: When You Can't Make Your House Payments, Is It Nearly Impossible to Avoid Foreclosure? ----------------------- 23

Tip # 10: Do Foreclosure Sales Offer a Good Opportunity to Buy a House at a Bargain Price? -------------------------------- 39

Summary -- 41

Free Bonus Gifts --- 42

Resources by H. Richard Steinhoff ------------------------------ 43

INTRODUCTION

Foreclosure is a legal process by which the lender takes back ownership of a property from a defaulted buyer. This process is different in every state and, in different locales, can take anywhere from 32 days to a year. The norm is about 120 days. A typical foreclosure timeline (representing California law) is illustrated in Figure 1.1.

According to real estate economists, the number of bank-owned properties is expected to gradually decline over the next three to five years. Clearly, foreclosures are going to be with us for a very long time.

This book will cover the details of foreclosures, and how they affect homeowners. It will give you tips on how to avoid foreclosure and foreclosure scams, the best time to buy in the foreclosure cycle, and how to minimize problems.

Tip # 1: Can You Make Money by Buying Bank Repossession (REO)?

An REO (Real Estate Owned) property is one that goes back to the lender after an unsuccessful foreclosure auction. The bank now owns the property, and the loan no longer exists. The bank will normally evict any occupants and may or may not make some repairs.

An REO is typically not a great bargain because the lender has incurred significant costs in foreclosing and is looking to recover those costs. In addition, you may have to make substantial repairs to put the property in marketable condition.

> BONUS TIP: Do Your Homework Before Buying an REO.

Figure 1.1: Foreclosure Action Timeline19 (California)

```
Day 1 ---------------------- Record Notice of
                             Default
Within 10 days--------------Mail Notice of Default
                             Public Notice of
                             Default
                             when Necessary
Within 1 month -------------Mail Notice of Default
After 3 months ------------- Set Sale Date
25 days before sale date ---Send Notice of Sale to
                             IRS—when Necessary,
20 days before sale date ---Public Notice of Sale
                             Post Notice of Sale
                             Mail Notice of Sale,
                             California
Within 10 days from first publication notice of sale -----Request
for directions
                             to property sent to
                             beneficiary
14 days before sale date ----- Request Notice of Sale
7 days before sale date ----Trustee cannot sell for 7
                             days after expiration of
                             court orders

5 business days before

sale date---------------------Right to reinstate

Sale date --------------------Sold!
```

Harry and Pam were experienced buyers, having moved several times. They were introduced to our agent, Sharon, to help them buy a house. They were well qualified and were looking in the $500,000 to $600,000 price range. They had also heard that you could save a lot of money by buying a bank-owned property, so they asked Sharon to find one for them.

After looking at several homes, they found one they wanted to buy. The bank had just taken the property back and had made no repairs. That suited Harry; he figured they could get a better price that way. The house was in pretty rough condition, but it was in a good neighborhood. It was listed at $610,000, so they offered $550,000. After several counter-offers, they accepted a price of $580,000.

After conducting a property inspection, they found that the home needed new flooring, window coverings, all new appliances, and a paint job, both inside and out. Harry figured that they were still all right because they were $30,000 below the asking price.

Once they closed the sale, they started getting estimates for all the repairs. As it turned out, the carpet cost $4,500, drapes $5,400, appliances $5,200, painting $3,900, repair of cabinets and other items $6,500, and replacing baseboards $2,800, for a grand total of $36,300. Harry and Pam had now invested $616,300.

They could have purchased a similar house needing no work for $610,000.

TIP # 2: ARE FORECLOSED HOMES FOUND ONLY IN BAD NEIGHBORHOODS?

Foreclosed properties are appearing more frequently in upscale neighborhoods. There was a recent bank-owned property for sale in our area for $12.9 million. It was previously owned by a Hollywood personality. Apparently, no one is immune from the recession.

Tip # 3: When Buying a House during the Foreclosure Process, is It Best to Buy in the Pre-Foreclosure Position?

Pre-foreclosure is the period between when the notice of default is filed and the property is sold at auction. Tip # 10 explains why you may not want to buy a property at a foreclosure sale. Therefore, if you absolutely must have a foreclosure, this is the best time to buy. The benefit here is that you are dealing directly with the homeowner, which is always the better choice. Depending upon his situation, the homeowner may be able to execute a short sale, which would be to your benefit.

Tip # 4: Will a Foreclosure Adversely Affect Your Credit?

According to www.myFICO.com, our clients, and other sources, your credit score could drop up to 200 points after a foreclosure and it will remain on your credit report for seven years.

This clearly is not a good alternative. There are better options.

CREDIT SCORE

720-850

700-719

675-699

620-674

560-619

500-559

Tip # 5: Do Foreclosed Homes Always Need a Lot of Work?

Some banks will completely rehab their REOs; others will just do cosmetic work, such as paint and carpeting. A few will do absolutely nothing. It all depends on the lender.

Tony and Linda were working with our agent, Mike, to find a home. They were a young couple just getting started and had limited resources. Mike showed them a newer neighborhood in their price range that consisted mostly of younger people with small children. There wasn't much on the market, and nothing they saw appealed to them.

About a week after their first outing, Mike called Tony and Linda with the news that a new listing just came on the market, but it was a bank-owned property. Tony and Linda were skeptical because they had heard that bank-owned properties were usually pretty rough, and they had no extra money to handle repairs. They figured, however, that it wouldn't hurt to look, so Mike took them to see the house.

When they opened the door, it was like an episode from *Extreme Makeover, Home Edition*. Linda shrieked and started crying. Tony kept saying, "Oh my gosh, Oh my gosh." The bank had completely rehabbed the house! It had new carpeting, new entry tile, new kitchen cabinets, countertops, flooring, and all the built-in appliances had been replaced. The house had been repainted, inside and out. It looked like a brand-new home. Tony and Linda could move right in without spending a dime. They immediately made a full-price offer of $385,000, which the bank accepted.

Forty-five days later, they moved in, still amazed at their good fortune—and thankful for Mike.

Tip # 6: Do Foreclosures Affect your Ability to Buy Another House?

According to Freddie Mac, the wait to buy another home is five years after the completed foreclosure sale. If you were an investor, or didn't live in the home, the wait is seven years. To make a loan after a foreclosure, lenders are looking for re-established credit with a FICO score of at least 680.

Tip # 7: Does a Homeowner Has a Redemption Period after a Foreclosure Sale Where He Can Regain Title to His Home?

Sometimes true, sometimes not. The redemption period varies from state to state. Some states have no redemption period, others allow up to a year. Most require you to pay all past-due payments, plus costs, to redeem your home. This is another reason to be careful if you are going to buy an REO.

Tip # 8: Can I Stay in My House for 30 Days after the Bank Has Repossessed It?

The Federal Protecting Tenants at Foreclosure Act (PTFA) provides that bona fide tenants are entitled to continue renting their homes for the duration of their lease after a foreclosure. In addition, new owners are required to give month-to-month tenants a minimum of 90 days notice prior to eviction.

The only exception is when the new owner intends to occupy the property as a primary residence. Then, the tenants can be required to vacate prior to the end of the lease with a 90 days' notice.

Former owners and tenants who receive government subsidies are not considered bona fide tenants.

PTFA was effective through December 31, 2014.

> BONUS TIP: Contact Your Lender before They Have Taken Ownership and Find Out What Their Eviction Policy Is. You Might Be Able to Stay Longer.

TIP # 9: WHEN YOU CAN'T MAKE YOUR HOUSE PAYMENTS, IS IT NEARLY IMPOSSIBLE TO AVOID FORECLOSURE?

There are many options to pursue before you got to foreclosure.[1]

1. Home Affordable Refinance Program (HARP) – Offers a new loan with lower interest rates and payments. (See Figure 1.2)

2. Repayment Plan – You can repay past-due amounts in a payment plan over time, in addition to your regular payment.

3. Forbearance – the lender reduces or suspends mortgage payments temporarily. The amount is usually added on to the end of the loan.

4. Loan Modification (HAMP) – reduces interest rate and payments. (See Figure 1.3)

5. Short Sale – You sell your home for less than the mortgage balance, and the lender takes a discount. Use the Home Affordable Foreclosure Alternatives Program (HAFA), if possible

---

[1] U.S. Department of the Treasury

6. Deed-in-Lieu of Foreclosure – The lender accepts transfer of title in exchange for cancelling the mortgage debt. Some additional tips to avoid foreclosure are provided in Figure 1.4.

In August 2010, the U. S. Treasury Department announced that it would provide $2 billion to 17 states that have unemployment rates higher than the national average, in order to aid the unemployed and help them save their homes from foreclosure. The program, called the Housing Finance Agency Innovation Fund for the Hardest Hit Housing Markets (HHF), will provide funding to the eligible states from the Federal Housing Finance Agency. (HFA)

Another $1 billion will go to the U.S. Department of Housing and Urban Development (HUD) for a new program that will provide homeowners with emergency loans of up to $50,000, with no interest or payments for up to two years. There really are a lot of options. Take advantage of them.

Figure 1.2: Home Affordable Refinance Program (HARP)[2]

To be eligible, you must meet the following requirements:

1. You must be the owner-occupant of your home.

2. Your loan must be guaranteed by Fannie Mae or Freddie Mac

3. You must be current on your mortgage payment.

4. You must have had no late payments in the last 6 months, and only one late payment in the last 12 months.

5. Your loan must have originally sold to Fannie Mae or Freddie Mac prior to May 31, 2009.

HARP's objective is to provide homeowners who have good credit an opportunity to reduce their payments with a new loan. The program expires on December 31, 2016. To find out if you have a Fannie Mae or Freddie Mac loan, ask your lender or call:

1-800-7 FANNIE for Fannie Mae, or

1- 800- FREDDIE for Freddie Mac

8 a.m. to 8 p.m., Eastern Standard Time

---

[2] U.S. Department of the Treasury

In 2012, The U. S. Justice Department announced a $25 Billion settlement with 5 major lenders, Bank of America, Wells Fargo, Ally Financial; J. P. Morgan Chase, and Bank of America, for improper foreclosure procedures.

$17 billion to be used for reducing principle balances of homeowners who owe more than their home is worth.

$5 billion to be used to pay $1800 to each homeowner who lost their home do to deceptive foreclosure practices.

$3 billon to be used to help homeowners refinance

The lenders are now in the process of carrying out the terms of this settlement.

Figure 1.3: Home Affordable Modification Program (HAMP)[3]

HAMP is designed to help homeowners struggling to avoid foreclosure by modifying their loan so that they can make their payments over the long term.

Eligibility requirements are:

1. Mortgage was originated prior to January 1, 2009

2. Principle loan balance less than $625,500.

3. Total monthly payment, including taxes and insurance, exceeds 31 percent of gross income

4. Home is occupied by the owner as a primary residence

5. Owner has a financial hardship and is delinquent on the mortgage

To reduce the owner's mortgage payment to less than 31 percent of his income, the lender will reduce the interest rate to as low as 2 percent and may extend the loan up to 40 years. The lender may also defer some of the principal until the end of the loan.

---

[3] U.S. Department of Housing and Urban Development

Effective June 1, 2012, the government expanded HAFA eligibility to include:

1. Homeowners who have rented their property or are intending to rent it.

2. Homeowners who previously did not qualify because their debt-to-income ratio was 31% or below.

3. Homeowners who previously received a HAMP trial period plan, but defaulted on it.

4. Homeowners who previously received a HAMP permanent modification, but defaulted on their payments.

Figure 1.4: Tips to Avoid Foreclosure[4]

1. Don't Ignore the Problem

The further behind you become, the more likely you that will lose your home.

2. Contact Your Lender Right Away

Lenders don't want your house, and they have options. Call them.

3. Open and Respond to all Mail from Your Lender

This is very important. Missing deadlines could cause you to lose your home.

4. Know Your Rights

Learn all about the foreclosure laws and time frames in your state.

5. Understand Your Options

They are outlined in Myth # 45.

6. Contact a HUD-Approved Housing Counselor

Call 1-800-569-4287 to find one near you.

7. Prioritize Your Spending

After healthcare, make house payments your first priority.

---

[4] U.S. Department of Housing and Urban Development

8. Use Your Assets

Sell whatever you can to pay your mortgage.

9. Avoid Foreclosure-Prevention Companies

HUD will provide a free counselor; don't pay for help.

10. Don't Lose Your Home to a Foreclosure-Recovery Scam

Review list of scams that follows

Avoid Foreclosure Scams.

Some of the more common scams are:[5]

1. Lease-Back Scheme – You are asked to transfer title to your home to the scammer who will, supposedly, obtain new financing, allow you to remain in the home as a renter, and eventually allow you to buy it back. All they want is your house and your money.

2. Fake "Government" Modification Programs – The scammer will claim to be affiliated with, or approved by, a government agency and require you to pay high up-front fees. You do not have to pay for legitimate government programs.

3. Bankruptcy Scams – The scammer will encourage you to file for bankruptcy, saying, "It's the only way …" Filing for bankruptcy is rarely, if ever, a permanent solution to prevent foreclosure. In addition, it will negatively impact your credit score and remain on your credit report for 10 years.

4. Debt-Elimination Schemes – The scammer will tell you to stop paying your mortgage, and they will be able to eliminate your debts. Don't stop making your payments.

5. Foreclosure "Rescue" and Refinance Fraud – The scam artist offers to act as an intermediary between you

---

[5] U.S. Department of the Treasury

and the lender to negotiate a loan modification. He usually asks for a large up-front fee. See Figure 1.5 for more warning signs.

Figure 1.5: Ten Warning Signs of a Mortgage Modification Scam[6]

1. "Pay us $1,000 and we'll save your home."

Some legitimate housing counselors may charge small fees, but fees that amount to thousands of dollars are likely a sign of potential fraud—especially if they are charged up-front, before the "counselor" has done any work for you. Be wary of companies that require you to provide a cashier's check or wire transfer before they take any action on your behalf.

2. "I guarantee I will save your home-trust me."

Beware of guarantees that a person or company can stop foreclosure and allow you to remain in your house. Unrealistic promises are a sign that the person making them will not consider your particular circumstances and is unlikely to provide services that will actually help you.

3. "Sign over your home, and we'll let you stay in it."

Be very suspicious if someone offers to pay your mortgage and rent your home back to you in exchange for transferring title to your home. Signing over the deed to another person gives that person the power to evict you, raise your rent, or sell the house. Although you will no longer own your home, you still will be legally responsible for paying the mortgage on it.

4. "Stop paying your mortgage."

Do not trust anyone who tells you to stop making payments to your lender and servicer, even if that person says it will be done for you.

---

[6] U.S. Department of the Treasury

5. "If your lender calls, don't talk to them."

Your lender should be your first point of contact for negotiating a repayment plan, modification, or short sale. It is vital to your interests to stay in close communication with your lender and servicer, so they understand your circumstances.

6. "Your lender never had the legal authority to make a loan."

Do not listen to anyone who claims that "secret laws" or "secret information" will be used to eliminate your debt and have your mortgage contract declared invalid. These scammers use sham legal arguments to claim that you are not obligated to pay your mortgage. These arguments don't work. **7. "Just sign this now; we'll fill in the blanks later."**

Take the time to read and understand anything you sign. Never let anyone else fill out paperwork for you. Don't let anyone pressure you into signing anything that you don't agree with or understand.

8. "Call 1-800-Fed-Loan."

This may be a scam. Some companies trick borrowers into believing that they are affiliated with or are approved by the government, or tell you that you must pay them high fees to qualify for government loan modification programs. Keep in mind that you do not have to pay to participate in legitimate government programs. All you need to do is contact your lender to find out if you qualify.

Figure 1.5: Ten Warning Signs of a Mortgage Modification Scam (continued)

9. "File for bankruptcy and keep your home."

Filing for bankruptcy only temporarily stops foreclosure. If your mortgage payments are not made, the bankruptcy court will eventually allow your lender to foreclose on your home. Be aware that some scammers will file bankruptcy in your name, without your knowledge, to temporarily stop foreclosure and make it seem as though they have negotiated a new payment agreement with your lender.

10. "Why haven't you replied to our offer? Do you want to live on the streets?"

High-pressure tactics signal trouble. If someone continually contacts you and pressures you to work with them to stop foreclosure, do not work with that person. Legitimate housing counselors do not conduct business that way.

Modification Scam[7]

Protect Yourself from Scams -- Below are a few ways to protect yourself from mortgage modification and foreclosure avoidance scams:

• **Contact your lender first** – Call the loss mitigation department to find out your alternatives.

• **Make all mortgage payments directly to your lender** – Do not trust anyone to do it for you, and do not stop making payments.

• **Avoid paying up-front fees** – Do not pay fees to anyone before receiving services. Make sure you are dealing with a legitimate organization.

• **Know what you are signing** – Read and understand every document you sign. Do not rely on oral explanations. Never sign anything with blank spaces to be filled in later! If you don't understand it, have a lawyer review it.

• **Do not sign your deed without consulting an attorney** –- Scams often involve transfer of ownership of your home to a scammer. By signing over your deeds you lose all rights to your home, and any equity you may have.

---

[7] U.S. Department of the Treasury

• **Get Promises in Writing** – Oral promises are not legally binding. Protect your rights with a legal document. Keep copies of all contracts you sign.

• **Report suspicious activity to federal agencies** – Call the Federal Trade Commission, or your state and local consumer protection agencies. This will also help prevent others from becoming victims.

• **Contact a legitimate housing or financial counselor to help you work it out** – To find a counselor, contact the U.S. Department of Housing and Urban Development (HUD) at: 1(800)569-4287 or 1(877)483-1515.

> BONUS TIP: *Always Proceed with Caution When Dealing with Anyone Offering to Help You Modify Your Mortgage or Avoid Foreclosure.*

Tip # 10: Do Foreclosure Sales Offer a Good Opportunity to Buy a House at a Bargain Price?

It's a very hard, if not impossible, to find a bargain at a foreclosure sale. In order to compete at the auction, you must have a cashier's check for the amount of your bid. If you are the successful bidder, you will receive the property in "as-is" condition, which could include someone living in the property. There may also be other liens on the property.

Foreclosure sales begin with a minimum bid that includes the loan balance, any accrued interest, attorney fees, and all other related costs. The minimum bid is typically more than the market value of the home. Since buyers are all looking for a bargain, the property usually reverts to the lender and becomes an REO.

There are some additional challenges in buying at auction:[8]

1. You will have limited or no access to the property because it is usually occupied

---

[8] Reprinted with permission of the Real Estate Buyer's Agent Council (REBAC), a wholly owned subsidiary of the National Association of Realtors. Copyright 2009, REBAC

2. After the sale, you may have to take legal action to evict the residents

3. You will not be able to conduct a property inspection

4. You are responsible for paying any outstanding liens

5. You may have an issue with borrower's right of redemption if you live in a state that allows it

6. The lender will require an all-cash, 30 day close

There many ways to save money when buying a house, but this isn't one of them.

Summary

You want to avoid foreclosure at all costs, because of the negative effect on your credit, plus you won't be able to buy another house for a very long time.

If you are facing foreclosure, there are a lot of options available to you, but you must follow the "New Rules" of real estate.

Rule # 1. Explore ALL your options.

Rule # 2. First, look into a HARP refinance program or a HAMP loan modification program..

Rule # 3. Next, try for a short sale.

Rule # 4. Avoid foreclosure scams at all costs.

If you would like to stay on the cutting edge of real estate, feel free to sign up for my newsletter at:

http://www.realestateinsidersguide.com

Best wishes in all your endeavors,

H. Richard Steinhoff

FREE BONUS GIFTS

As a thank-you for purchasing **Real Estate Investing 101:Best New Foreclosure Solutions**, H. Richard Steinhoff is offering you the following free gifts:

• **How to Find the Best Mortgage**

A report to assist you in obtaining the best mortgage for your situation, including a two page Mortgage Shopping Worksheet

• **Buying and Financing Guide for Homebuyers**

A report covering all aspects of buying and financing a home, including a detailed explanation of settlement (closing) costs and settlement (closing) statements

This report is invaluable to potential homebuyers

To claim your free gifts, go to:

www.realestateinsidersguide.com/bookbonus.html

Resources by H. Richard Steinhoff

Real Estate Investing 101: Best Way to Buy a House and Save Big, Top 20 Tips (Volume 1)

Real Estate Investing 101: Best Way to Sell a House Fast for Top Dollar, Top 14 Tips (Volume 2)

Real Estate Investing 101: Best Way to Save Money on a Good Home Loan, Top 13 tips (Volume 3)

Real Estate Investing 101: Best New Short Sale Solutions, Top 10 Tips (Volume 4)

Real Estate Investing 101: Best New Foreclosure Solutions, Top 10 Tips (Volume 5)

Real Estate Investing 101: Best Way to Invest for Big Returns, Top 10 Tips (Volume 6)

Real Estate Investing 101: Best Way to Find a Good Real Estate Agent, Top 13 Tips. (Volume 7)

Turning Myths into Money: An Insider's Guide to Winning the Real Estate Game

www.ingramcontent.com/pod-product-compliance
Ingram Content Group UK Ltd.
Pitfield, Milton Keynes, MK11 3LW, UK
UKHW022218230426
12048UKWH00016BA/919